BEHIND THE MASS

A Sequel to *Let Holy Mass Be Your Life*

by

Rev. Albert Joseph Mary Shamon

Published by

THE RIEHLE FOUNDATION

P. O. Box 7

Milford, Ohio 45150

Imprimatur: ✠ Matthew H. Clark
                Bishop of Rochester, NY
                January 11, 1995

Published by The Riehle Foundation

For additional copies, write:

The Riehle Foundation
P.O. Box 7
Milford, Ohio 45150

Library of Congress Catalog Card No.: 95-067168

ISBN: 1-877678-34-1

CONTENTS

DEDICATION

I dedicate *Behind the Mass* to a very great woman and a dearly beloved friend:

Frances Riehle Reck
The Riehle Foundation
(1933-1994)

Frances was one of the foremost evangelists of our times through her printed word and her writings.

In her gentle and unobtrusive way, she touched the hearts of thousands.

Like Mary, the Mother of God, she was a woman wrapped in silence. Like Mary, to whom she was consecrated, she served the Lord in hiddenness. Like Mary, too, her achievements were great—through her, God did great things.

Her life was gentle and all the elements so mixed in her that nature might stand up and say to all the world, "This was a woman!"

PREFACE

This booklet is a sequel to *Our Lady Says: Let Holy Mass Be Your Life.*

I called it *Behind the Mass,* because it deals in great part with the theology of the Mass.

It supplements *Let Holy Mass Be Your Life.* Both booklets will give Catholics and Protestants, converts, and those in RCIA classes, a fundamental grasp of the Most Holy Eucharist, which is the center of the whole Christian life.

*   *   *

The revised Code of Canon Law gives a beautiful definition of the Most Holy Eucharist. Here it is:

> The Most Holy Eucharist is the most august **sacrament,** in which Christ the Lord Himself is *contained, offered and received,* and by which the Church constantly lives and grows (Canon 897).

The **Most Holy Eucharist** has four other names, depending on the angle from which we view it. Just as when we study man's mind, we have the science of psychology; when we study his body, anatomy; his thinking, logic, etc., so with the Eucharist. When we view the Eucharist as *containing* the Body and Blood of Christ, we call it the **Blessed Sacrament.** When we view it as being *offered,* we call it the **Mass.** When we view it as being *received* during life, we call it **Holy Communion**; and when we view it as being *received* when dying, we call it **Holy Viaticum**—food "with" *(cum)* "you" *(ti)* on the "journey" *(via)* to eternity.

We shall treat the Mass first (Christ as victim) then the Blessed Sacrament (Christ as companion), and finally Holy Communion (Christ as food).

Feast of the Presentation of Mary
November 21, 1994
Albert Joseph Mary Shamon

Chapter 1

WHAT IS THE MASS?

After the consecration of the Mass, the priest says, "Let us proclaim the mystery of faith." I have asked people again and again, what is the mystery of faith that we proclaim. Often, they will say, "Christ has died, Christ is risen, Christ will come again."

Yes, it is true that the mystery of faith, broadly speaking, is the Paschal mystery of Christ's Passion, Death, Resurrection, Ascension and eventual return in glory which He underwent out of love for us and for our salvation. But more particularly, the mystery of faith we wish to focus on here is the presence of the risen Christ on our altars after the consecration.

The Mass is simply the prayerful celebration of the mystery of Christ's *presence* in the midst of His people.

First of all, the Mass is a celebration. The priest doesn't say Mass; he celebrates Mass. **Celebration** is the joyful sharing of a happy event. Every celebration has three elements.

First, there has to be a **happy event** to have

1

a celebration; for instance, a wedding, a birth-day, a graduation, an ordination, a holiday like the Fourth of July, and so on.

The Mass celebrates a happy event: the coming of the risen Christ to our altars. Imagine, it is not the President of the United States who comes. No! It is the King of kings, the Lord of lords. And He comes, not so much to be adored, not to condemn us, but for the same reason He came 2,000 years ago; namely, to show us He loves us, to guide us, to heal us, to help us, to save us, to build up a friendship with us. Doesn't that call for celebration? It sure does!

Then for a celebration, there has to be a **sharing.** Shared joy is double joy. Smarty could not have his party, because nobody came. To celebrate, we need people. In fact the word "celebration" comes from the Latin word *cele-ber,* which means "people," "a crowd."

That is one of the reasons why deliberately missing Sunday Mass is a mortal sin: we can't properly celebrate without people; and people cannot be saved without Christ. Hence the author of *The Letter to the Hebrews* wrote, "*We must not stay away from our assembly as is the custom of some, but encourage one another.*" (*Hebrews* 10:25).

The gathering at Sunday Mass is, among other things, a support community—an encouragement to others.

Finally, a celebration ought to be **joyful,** for the event that is celebrated is a happy one. How ignorant of what the Mass is are those who gripe and carp because they "have to" go to Sunday Mass! We ought to run to Mass, not creep like a snail. The Mass opens with song; it climaxes by offering us the Bread of Life; it has all the trappings of festivity. It is an action of joy.

The Mass is the joyful celebration of the presence of Christ in the midst of His people. The key to understanding the new order of the Mass is that of **presence.**

Vatican II in its *Constitution on the Sacred Liturgy* (#7) says:

> . . .Christ is always present in His Church, especially in her liturgical celebrations. He is present in the sacrifice of the Mass, not only in the person of His ministers. . .but especially under the Eucharistic species. . .He is present in His word. . .He is present, finally, when the Church prays and sings, for He promised, *"where two or three are gathered together for my sake, there am I in the midst of them" (Matthew* 18:20).

To celebrate these four presences of Christ in the Mass, the Mass has four movements, like a great symphony. The first movement in the Mass is the Introductory Rites; the second, the

Liturgy of the Word; the third, the Liturgy of the Eucharist; and the fourth, the Concluding Rite.

The first movement in the Mass, the Introductory Rites, celebrates the **General Presence** of Christ at Mass.

Take a boy and girl, we'll call them Joseph and Mary. They are madly in love with each other. They want to get married, but their parents nix their desire. They insist that Mary first finish college and that Joseph finish his boot training in the armed forces. So Mary goes to college and Joe to army camp. They are separated. But are they not still on each other's minds and in each other's hearts? Are they not still present to each other in thought and desire? In fact, maybe that is all Joe talks about to the other guys—about his Mary. And no doubt Joe is all that Mary fantasizes, dreams and moons about—her Joe.

That is what we mean by General Presence: the presence of lovers in each other's minds and hearts. As the song puts it, "Gentle on my mind."

At Mass we are gathered together in the name of Christ. That is what the Introductory Rites are all about: they gather us together in the name of Jesus.

Thus when the priest comes down the aisle to begin Mass, we greet him with song, just as fans cheer their team when they run out on the football field. One of these entrance songs expresses accurately why we gather together:

We gather together to sing the Lord's praises. To worship the Father through Jesus His Son. In this celebration, all sing in jubilation! We are His holy people whose freedom He won.

Secondly, because our gathering together in the name of Jesus makes Him present in our midst, the Penitential Rite immediately follows the Greeting. For Christ is the light; and in His light, we can see our imperfections. So, like Peter, we too cry out, *"Depart from me, Lord, for I am a sinful man" (Luke* 5:8)—that is what we are doing when we say three times, "Lord, have mercy."

But we stop at that. This rite is brief. St. Thomas, in writing about meditation, asks the question: "About what should we meditate?" He answers that we should meditate on self and on God; but not too much on self, lest it lead to despair. So the liturgy does not let us linger too long on our sins, lest we become discouraged.

Thus immediately after our confession of sinfulness comes the Glory to God. We praise the Father for sending the Lamb of God Who takes away the sin of the world.

Remember, the Mass is a **prayerful** celebration. So this first movement of the Mass concludes and climaxes with the Opening Prayer. This Prayer suggests the particular grace we should ask for at each Mass. Each Sunday we should come to Mass early so that we can open the Missalette and read this Prayer to discover what grace we should be asking for.

The second movement of the Mass is the Liturgy of the Word. This movement celebrates the **Verbal Presence** of the risen Christ in our midst.

Let us recall our two lovers: Joseph in boot camp and Mary in college. Are they content just to dream about each other? We all know better. They write letters to each other; and when he's got enough money, he calls her on the phone. She in turn writes and phones. They do this, because this is a greater presence than merely by thought and by desire. That is what Verbal Presence is—presence by letter or by word.

Likewise, God is not content to be present to us only as the beloved is in the mind of the lover. Oh no! He wants to be verbally present to us. So God the Father writes to us in the Old Testament. God the Son writes to us in the New Testament. And God the Holy Spirit speaks to us in the homily.

After each of the Sunday readings we do not say, "This is the word *about* the Lord." No way. Rather, we simply say, "The word *of* the Lord." St. Augustine said, "When we pray, we speak to God. When we read, God speaks to us."

And boy, that ought to make us happy! That calls for celebration. After all our coldness and indifference to God, He still speaks to us. He doesn't give us the silent treatment that husbands and wives often give each other after they have quarreled. Young lovers, if they quarrel, often do the same thing: they stop talking or writing to each other. But not God. He loves us with an everlasting love. His love for us never changes. That calls for an "Alleluia!"—a "Praise the Lord!"

When God talks to us, what should we do? We should be *listening*. That's elementary courtesy. That was why Jesus didn't give Martha the time of day when He was visiting her and Mary and Lazarus. She was busy about many things while He was there. She wasn't listening to Him as Mary was. For that discourtesy, Jesus sided with Mary.

Besides listening, one must act on the word: *"Be doers of the word and not hearers only"* (*James* 1:22).

Sometimes people say, "I don't get anything out of the Mass." Well, here's a good place to start. Some kids don't get anything out of school. Because they don't pay attention in school. So here, pay attention to God's words. Listen to them. Remember, Christ likened His word to seed and us to soil. Whether or not the seed produces fruit depends on the soil. In computer language, "The receiver controls input." St. Anthony Mary Claret taught: "When we go to Holy Communion, all of us receive the same Lord Jesus, but not all receive the same grace... Our differences in disposition is the reason."

Again, this second movement of the Mass, like the first, climaxes in prayer: the General Intercessions. These prayers are most important, for they are the prayers of the Mystical Body of Christ.

The third movement of the Mass is the Liturgy of the Eucharist. This movement celebrates the **Real Presence** of Jesus in our midst.

This movement of the Mass is subdivided into three parts, because it is modeled on the words and actions of Jesus at the Last Supper. At the Last Supper, Jesus did three things: (1) He took bread and wine—this is done at the **Preparation of the Gifts**; (2) He gave thanks—this is done in the **Eucharist Prayer** (there are four or more of them for variety and to prevent formalism); and (3) He said, *"Take and eat"*—this is done at **Communion** time.

Again, see how truly the Mass is a **prayerful** celebration. The Preparation of the Gifts concludes with a Prayer over the Gifts; and the Communion, with a Prayer after Communion; whereas the core of the Mass, the Eucharistic Prayer, is all prayer.

After His three actions at the Last Supper, Jesus did a fourth thing. He said, *"Do this in remembrance of me."* Why?

To remember is to think of; to think of is to be thankful for. The words "think" and "thank" differ only by single vowel.

The sin of the angels was pride; the sin of man is amnesia. Jesus commanded us to think of what He had done for us so that we might love Him and be thankful to Him. St. Paul told the early Christians again and again to give thanks to God for having called them from death to life, from darkness to light, from slavery to freedom—all this, through no merit of their own, but through the sheer grace of God.

That is why the early Christians changed the name of the Mass from "the Breaking of the Bread" to the "Eucharist"—"the Thanksgiving." If we want one reason for going to

Mass, it is that we ought to say "thank you" to God for loving us so much and for giving us so much.

Recall our two lovers Joseph and Mary. They had dreamed of each other; they had written to each other, talked on the phone. But at long last he finishes his training in boot camp; and she, her courses in college. They come home. We can well imagine the joy of their meeting, the ardor of their embraces. Now they are really present to each other.

So at the Mass, at the consecration, the risen Jesus truly, really and substantially comes to the altar. The mystery of faith is this **Real Presence** of Christ on our altars after the consecration.

So really and truly present is our Lord that the Church ordered that the tabernacle be taken off the altar of sacrifice. The reason is that the Mass celebrates the bringing of Christ to our altars. If He is already on the altar, then the meaning of the Mass could be blurred.

Thus the Sacred Congregation of Rites wrote:

In the celebration of Mass the principal modes of Christ's presence to His Church emerge clearly one after the other: first He is seen to be present in the assembly of the faithful gathered in His name; then in His word, with the reading. . .of Scripture; also in the person of the minister; finally, in a singular way under the Eucharistic elements. Consequently, on the grounds of the sign value, it is more in keeping with the nature of the celebration that, through reservation of the sacrament in the tabernacle, Christ not be present Eucharistically from the beginning on the altar where Mass is celebrated. That presence is the effect of the consecration and should appear as such. (*Instruction on Eucharistic Worship*, 5/25/67, #55).

To demonstrate the reality of this presence, after the consecration, the priest elevates the Host so that people can make an act of faith in His presence; and then he immediately genuflects as a testimony to his belief in Christ's presence.

The Eucharistic Acclamation follows. Since the Acclamation is addressed to Christ present on the altar, it should always be in the second person. Thus "dying **you** destroyed our death." When a team comes on the field, they are acclaimed; we don't talk about them, we acclaim them.

I used to wonder why the words of consecration were always enshrined in the narrative of the Last Supper. Then one day it hit me like a flash of light.

Time and tide, you see, wait for no man. Time just flows on. Philosophers define time as the *nunc fluens*—the "flowing now." If we stand in front of a fast-flowing stream, the water in front of us is gone almost the very instant it is present before us. So it is with time. The present is but an instant; it moves on much like the second hand on a watch. The present instant is gone almost as soon as it is present. No one can stop time.

How can we triumph over this tyranny of time? By a wonderful faculty God has given us: **memory**. Memory can regroup these scattered instances, bring the past back to the present. Memory can make the past present again.

Memories, however are only ideal—that is, they are the products of the mind and the imagination and do not exist outside of them. And yet there is much of reality in memories. In some movies—for instance *The Long Grey Line, Maytime* and *Goodbye, Mr. Chips,* to mention just a few oldies—the entire movie is a flashback, an old person reminiscing about his or her past. Though the recall of the past is real enough, yet the memories are still only a figment of the imagination.

Christ, however, because He is God, is not subject to such limitations. He can recall the past, not just in imagination, but actually and really, just as the phonograph can bring back the golden voices of Enrico Caruso and Mario Lanza.

Memory, you see, can recall past events and make them present—but only in the mind of the one remembering. However, Jesus promised that when we remember what He did at the Last Supper, this remembering would not only **recall** what He did then, but actually and truly **re-call** Him from Heaven to our altars—making Him present not just in our minds, but really, truly and substantially on our altars. The priest recalls Him to the altar as truly as a nation might recall her ambassador home.

Finally, when Joseph and Mary come home, what do they do? They marry. Their love leads to communion; the two become one. So Christ comes to our altars to enter into communion with us at Holy Communion.

The fourth and last movement of the Mass is the **Concluding Rite.** This celebrates the **Cosmic Presence** of Christ: making Him present in the world and to the world.

The first words of Jesus to His apostles were, *"Come, follow me."* His last were, *"Go, teach all nations."* So the Concluding Rite of the Mass is a mandate to mission.

After Joe and Mary had been married, in the normal course of events, they would bring children into the world. And they would impart to them their culture and religious world view.

Likewise, the priest ends the Mass with the commission to go. He says in effect, "Go! Go, now that you have been fed by the bread of the word of God and have been nourished by the bread of His Body and Blood. Go! Go into the world and make Christ present there. Penetrate the darkness of society by the light of the gospel truth; leaven it with the yeast of your good works; and season it with the salt of your good example."

His exact words are, "Go in peace to love and serve the Lord"—to love the Lord by serving your neighbor; and to serve the Lord by loving your neighbor in bringing to each one the good news of how much God loves them!

Chapter 2

WHY THE MASS?

The Mass is the celebration of Christ's presence in the midst of His people. Now we might ask, "Why does He become present?"

First of all, He does not come simply to be adored. This happens, of course, but oh how briefly, at the elevation of the Host and the Cup. Here is what Pius Parsch wrote in his *The Liturgy of the Mass*:

> The primary purpose of the Mass is not, of course, the adoration of the sacred species. This is merely secondary. It is to offer sacrifice—Christ's Sacrifice and ours. Besides adoring Christ in His real presence, our task at Mass is to offer Him, the divine Victim, to God the Father in Heaven. We stress this point because at one time the Mass tended to become in the eyes of the people merely an act of devotion in adoration of the Eucharist, and we feel that much work may still need to be done to bring about the necessary change of attitude in our own generation toward the Mass (p. 241).

Christ comes to our altars for the very same reason He came when He walked the earth; namely, to help us, to heal us, to save us.

How?

1. By enabling us to offer highest worship to the Father and thus to bring peace on earth through glory to God.

If the words of consecration are the two most important phrases in the Mass, the next two most important words are in the prayer following the Eucharistic Acclamation, namely, the words "**we offer.**" These words express *our* sacrifice. The Sacrifice of the Mass is not just Jesus offering Himself to the Father as He did on Calvary, but our offering ourselves with Him to the Father. That is one of the ways Calvary differs from the Mass. On Calvary Jesus sacrificed alone. At Mass our sacrifices are joined to His.

And what do we offer besides Christ? We offer our money at the collection, plus all the crosses that may have come our way during the preceding week. Just as water dilutes wine, so our offerings dilute Jesus' offering. That is why we pray: "Look with favor on your Church's offering . . ." (Eucharistic Prayer III). That would be blasphemous if what we offered were only Jesus, the spotless Lamb of God. Instead, we hide behind Jesus and ask the Father "see the Victim whose death has reconciled us to yourself."

A lady once objected to going to Mass on the grounds that she went to Holy Communion everyday. Why go to Mass? Precisely for this reason: to give glory to God and thus bring peace on earth.

2. The second reason for the Mass is to change us into loving persons. As bread and wine are changed into the Body and Blood of Christ, so Christ would change us into Himself. As Christ said to St. Augustine, "Thou wilt not change Me into thee as thou dost ordinary bread, but thou shalt be changed into Me."

In the Mass there are two invocations of the Holy Spirit.

One is made before the consecration, when the priest holds his hands over the gifts of bread and wine and prays to the Father: "Let your Spirit come upon these gifts to make them holy, so that they may become for us the Body and Blood of our Lord, Jesus Christ" (Eucharistic Prayer II).

Wow! What a request! When Gabriel announced to Mary that God wanted her to be the mother of His Son, and she said "Yes," the Son of God, the Word, was made flesh in her womb by the power of the Holy Spirit. She conceived by the Holy Spirit. So the Church asks that the same Holy Spirit be sent once again by the Father to repeat this miracle at every Mass; namely, to make the risen

Christ present in the "womb" of bread and wine. What a prayer!

And God always hears the prayers of His spouse, the Church. Her prayer is infallibly answered. At the consecratory words, He comes! Really and truly and substantially. The risen Christ. There is a hush. The Host is lifted. We pray, "My Lord and my God!" And the priest in silent adoration bends the knee.

Immediately, there follows the Acclamation and the Offertory—the sacrifice of the Mass.

Right after the Offertory, we invoke the Holy Spirit a second time. Before the consecration, we asked the Holy Spirit to change the bread and the wine into the **physical** Body of Christ. Now, after the consecration, we ask the Holy Spirit to change the congregation, assembled for Mass, into the **mystical** Body of Christ, the Church, by giving her the mark of unity.

At this point in the Mass, I generally hold my hands over the congregation, just as I do over the gifts of bread and wine before the consecration. While doing this, I utter, just as every other priest does at Mass, these words: "May all of us who share in the Body and Blood of Christ be brought together in **unity** by the Holy Spirit."

The bond of unity is love. Love is unitive: it makes two become one.

I used to think that love was something we can generate from within ourselves; that we could drill deep down into the innermost recesses of our hearts—and behold, love would gush forth, like oil from a well. If we could do that, we could easily love our enemies. But it is not that easy. As fuel has to be pumped into a car, so love has to be poured into us from outside ourselves.

Then where do we get love? From God, for God is love. And the service station from where love can be poured into the tanks of our hearts is the Mass. Thus in our prayer for unity, we ask that unity come to all who receive Holy Communion, the sacrament of love, by the Holy Spirit, the God of love. This double outpouring of love at every Mass, from Holy Communion and from the Holy Spirit, is the **sacramental grace** of the Mass.

One day after having celebrated Mass on a retreat with Eileen George, she said to us priests, "Fathers, I wish you could have seen what I saw at your Mass." Naturally, we asked her what she saw. She said, "I saw St. Michael the Archangel standing beside you priests, protecting you from the devil. Above you all, I saw Daddy God, with Mary at His side, surrounded by a host of angels and saints. Then I saw six angels go out from the altar, sprinkling above the congregation something that looked like gold dust. I asked the Father what they were doing." He answered that they were applying to the people the graces of the Mass.

Each and every Mass gives us the grace to become more and more loving. Each and every Mass is meant to transform us more and more into loving persons. Eventually, if all of us are open to this influx of love, the Christian community becomes a community of loving persons—becomes what the Church is meant to be. Thus St. Augustine wrote, "The Church makes the Eucharist, and the Eucharist makes the Church."

That is why daily Mass is so important: we need to have love poured into us day in and day out. As Burt Bacharach lyricized:

What the world needs now
Is love, sweet love.
It's the only thing
that there's just too little of.

Lord, we don't need another mountain.
There are mountains and hillsides,
    enough to climb;
There are oceans and rivers, enough to
    cross,
Enough to last until the end of time.

What the world needs now
Is love, sweet love.
It's the only thing
that there's just too little of.

Lord, we don't need another meadow,
There are cornfields and wheatfields,
   enough to grow.
There are sunbeams and moonbeams,
   enough to shine.
Oh, listen, Lord, if you wanna know:

What the world needs now
Is love, sweet love.
No, not just for some,
But for everyone!

Here are some stanzas from a poem by James Patrick Kinney, expressing how much loved is needed. He titled it *The Cold Within:*

Four humans trapped by happenstance
In bleak and bitter cold.
Each one possessed a stick of wood.
Or so the story's told.

Their dying fire in need of logs,
The first man held his back,
For of the faces round the fire,
He noticed one was black.

The next man looking cross the way
Saw one not of his church.
And couldn't bring himself to give
The fire his stick of birch.

The black man's face bespoke revenge
As the fire passed from his sight.
For all he saw in his stick of wood
Was a chance to spite the white.

The last man of this forlorn group
Did nought except for gain.
Giving only to those who gave
Was how he played the game.

Their logs held tight in death's still
   hands
Was proof of human sin.
They didn't die from the cold
   without;
They died from the cold within.

3. Finally, we are filled with love at every Mass that we might bring love to others.

There are four degrees of love. Just as those closer to a fire receive more of its heat, so those closest to us should receive more of our love.

Our first love, therefore, should be for our families; blood is thicker than water. The word *kind* comes from the word *kin* plus a *d*. Husbands must love their wives, wives their husbands, parents their children, and children their parents. Charity begins at home.

However, charity at home should spill over to our spiritual family—to those belonging to mother Church. Thus in the Eucharistic

Prayers, we pray for the Pope, bishops, priests, the souls in purgatory, and all the faithful present at Mass.

Next, our love must reach out to our neighbors. No man is an island. We owe other people. There was a television program titled *Ten Thousand People Make My Breakfast*—and that is so true. Thus Mass ends with the commission to "go in peace to love and serve the Lord"—to love Him by serving our neighbor; and to serve Him by loving our neighbor.

Lastly, our love must reach out to our enemies. As the intensity of a fire is measured by how far it throws its heat, so the degree of our love for God is measured by how wide is our embrace of love.

We love our enemies, not as enemies, but as creations of God, destined for Heaven; that is, as potential saints.

The mission of the Church, as Pope Paul VI said, is "to create a civilization of love."

At every Mass, Christ gives us a blank check, signed by Himself. How much we draw out depends on the amount we write in. What we "get out" of the Mass depends upon how much we put into it: our attention, our devotion, our desire. How much water we draw from a well will depend on the size of the bucket we bring to the well.

Pope John XXIII said, "Take away from the altar fire, not ashes—the fire of love, and zeal for souls."

*   *   *

"As the chosen of God, then, the holy people whom he loves, you are to be clothed in heartfelt compassion, in generosity and humility, gentleness and patience. Bear with one another; forgive each other if one of you has a complaint against another. The Lord has forgiven you; now you must do the same. Over all these clothes, put on love, the perfect bond. And may the peace of Christ reign in your hearts, because it is for this that you were called together in one body. Always be thankful.

"Let the Word of Christ, in all its richness, find a home with you. Teach each other, and advise each other, in all wisdom. With gratitude in your hearts sing psalms and hymns and inspired songs to God; and whatever you say or do, let it be in the name of the Lord Jesus, in thanksgiving to God the Father through him" (Colossians 3:12-17).

Chapter 3

TRANSUBSTANTIATION

We have already discussed the what and the why of the Mass. Now we wish to talk about the Most Holy Eucharist as containing the Body and Blood, Soul and Divinity of our Lord Jesus Christ; in other words, we want to discuss the Blessed Sacrament.

Our question is this: how can the Son of God be present in a wafer, not just on one altar, but on all altars throughout the world? How can this be? That's a humdinger of a question.

In the Middle Ages the best minds in the Church probed this question. Around A.D. 1050, Berengarius denied the real presence of Jesus in the Eucharist. This created a storm in Europe. One of Berengarius' most vigorous opponents was Heldebert of Tours (c. 1097). He seems to have been the first writer to employ the word "transubstantiation" to explain the presence of Christ in the Eucharist.

Berengarius was excommunicated, but died at peace with the Church in A.D. 1088. In A.D. 1215, the Fourth Lateran Council (with both St. Francis of Assisi and St. Dominic present) defined that "the bread is changed into His body by the divine power of transubstantiation" (BD #430).

The Church adopted the term "transubstantiation" officially at the Council of Trent. The Council declared:

> . . . by the consecration of the bread and wine there takes place a change of the whole substance of the bread into the substance of the body of Christ our Lord and of the whole substance of the wine into the substance of His blood. This change the holy Catholic Church has fittingly and properly called transubstantiation (quoted in the *Catechism of the Catholic Church* #1376).

Pope Paul VI in his encyclical *Mysterium Fidei* (9/3/65) wrote:

> . . . the way Christ is made present in this Sacrament is none other than by the change of the whole substance of the bread into His Body, and of the whole substance of the wine into His Blood, and that this unique and truly wonderful change the Catholic Church rightly calls transubstantiation (#46).

One priest said that we should not use such unfamiliar and arcane terminology as transubstantiation. James Likoudis soundly repri-manded him. Likoudis said:

> If the term transubstantiation is unfamiliar and arcane terminology, it is because too many pastors and religious educators have failed miserably to instruct the faithful properly concerning a term which safeguards the authentic meaning of the awesome mystery of the Eucharist (*Wanderer* 6/2/94).

Lest we also be guilty of neglecting our teaching mission, let me explain what is meant by transubstantiation.

First of all, transubstantiation does not explain *how* our Lord is present in the Blessed Sacrament. That is a mystery of faith. Transub-stantiation simply shows that the doctrine of His presence is not something contrary to reason.

Fr. Faber, while yet a Protestant, said:

> I am worried about the Roman doc-trine because whatever may be said of the proofs of it, I do not see how any man can disprove it. If they say that the substance changes, but that all appear-ances remain the same, then they say that something changes of which no man has any experience and yet which reason must postulate as the reality underlying

all appearances and separate from them. (Carty, *Quizzes*, #32).

Well, here's what Faber meant. Let's take any thing. Everything has two elements: a **visible** one: what can be seen or perceived by the senses—the **appearances;** and an **invisible** one: what cannot be seen or perceived by the senses—the **substance.**

Consider a bar of iron, for instance. These are its appearances: it is cold; black; rigid.

Now, put this bar of iron in a smelting furnace and melt it. In doing this, we change all its appearances. It is no longer shaped like a bar, but has the form of the receptacle in which it was melted; it is no longer cold, but hot; no longer black, but red; no longer rigid, but fluid.

In other words, we have changed all the appearances, and we still have iron.

Suppose I and my clothes were one: everytime I changed my clothes, I'd be changing me. But I can change my clothes and not myself, because I and my clothes are distinct.

Likewise, I can change all the appearances of iron and still have iron. What does that tell me? It says loud and clear, that there is something else in iron, besides the appearances— and that, that other something is precisely what makes it iron. That something else philosophers call *substance*—that which *stands under* the appearances of the thing and makes it what it is! The substance, not the appearances, make a thing what it really is. And so we speak of the essence, the heart, the substance of a thing.

Now, consider what we can do to the appearances and the substance of a thing.

We can, for instance, change the appearances of a thing and not the substance. We are always doing this. When we change the furniture in a room, when we paint a house, and so on, we are changing appearances, but not the substance. We call this a *cosmetic* change. Hamlet said to Ophelia, "God has given you one face, and you make yourselves another" (*Hamlet* Act 3, sc. 1, line 149).

We can also change both the appearances and the substance of a thing. In chemistry, we call this a chemical or substantial change; e.g., we can take two atoms of hydrogen and one of oxygen and use an electric spark and get water $(2H + O = H_2O)$—we are reducing two gases to a liquid. Whenever we smoke, we reduce a cigarette to gas and ash. These are substantial changes.

But we cannot change the substance of a thing and leave its appearances untouched. For instance, we cannot change a bar of iron into gold and still have it look like iron.

Jesus, however, showed He had the power to make such a change.

First, He could change the appearances of a thing and not its substance—anybody can do that.

Secondly, He could change both the appearances and the substance of a thing as He did at Cana of Galilee. There, He changed what looked like water and was water into what looked like wine and was wine.

And thirdly, He showed He could do what we cannot do, namely, change the substance of a thing and not its appearance. He did this when He multiplied five loaves and two fish to feed about 15,000 people (*John* 6:1-15).

It is significant that we refer to this miracle as the multiplying of the loaves of bread, and not as the creating of them.

What was Jesus doing? He was proving He could affect the substance of things without changing their appearances.

It is significant, too, that He used fish, and not wine, in this foreshadowing of the Eucharist, because the symbol of the fish was the sign Christians used in time of persecution to reveal to one another that they were Christians. Fish was a good symbol because the Greek word for fish, namely, *ichthus*, was an acrostic for "Jesus Christ Son of God Savior." So this miracle of the loaves and fish most aptly signified the Eucharist, in which consecrated bread contains Jesus Christ, Son of God, Savior.

It is also significant that after this miracle, Jesus walked on water, to show that He could do with His Body whatever He pleased.

In the context of these two miracles, Jesus asked for faith in Himself and promised the Eucharist. He promised to give His followers His Flesh to eat and His Blood to drink. But they refused to believe Him, to trust His words, and so most left Him—but not the Twelve. The Eucharist became the acid test of the true followers of Jesus.

One year later, at the Last Supper, Jesus fulfilled His promise. He took bread and said:

THIS—not bread, but this thing that looks like bread.

IS—not bread, but My Body. "Is" is a copulative, linking verb: this thing that looks like bread is not bread but My Body. "Is" means *is;* it does not mean contains or symbolizes, but *is* My Body.

MY BODY—here "Body" stands for "Me." "This is *Me!*"

31

Yet the bread still looks like bread. But Jesus said it isn't! By the great miracle of the loaves and fish, by His walking on water, He proved He could do it. He promised He would do it. At the Last Supper, He did do it.

But the bread still looked like bread and the wine still looked like wine. But Jesus said they were no longer bread and wine, but His Body and Blood. What happened?

The miracle of transubstantiation took place. Transubstantiation is the miracle whereby the substance of the bread changed into the Body of Christ and the substance of the wine into the Blood of Christ, the appearances alone remaining.

The outside stays the same; it changes on the inside.

Protestants called this "hocus pocus." This expression of theirs was a parody on the words of consecration at Mass. In Latin, the consecratory words are ***Hoc est enim corpus meum***—hocus pocus.

Catholics call it the "mystery of faith": *mystery*, because we cannot see the change; *of faith*, because we take the words of Jesus. He promised it, He could keep His promise and He did. On a button there was this inscription: "Jesus said it. I believe it. That settles it."

St. Thomas Aquinas in his hymn the *Adoro Te Devote* wrote:

Sight, touch and taste in Thee are each
  deceived
The ear alone most safely is believed.
I believe all the Son of God has spoken.
Than Truth's own words there is no
  truer token.

In the Dresden Art Gallery there is a tryptych picturing:

Luther   Christ   Calvin

Beneath each person are these words: under Luther, "This contains my body"; under Calvin, "This is my dynamic presence"; and under Christ, "This is My Body." Underneath these three inscriptions are the words: "Who speaks the truth?"

How is this miracle of transubstantiation effected? Not just by the words of consecration, but by the words of consecration uttered by a validly ordained priest, another Christ, one acting *in persona Christi*.

St. Thomas says that transubstantiation is "entirely supernatural, and effected by God's power alone." Then he quotes St. Ambrose:

See how Christ's word changes
nature's laws, as He wills: a man is not
wont to be born save of man and

woman: see therefore that against the established law and order a man is born of a Virgin... It is clear that a Virgin begot beyond the order of nature: and what we make is the body from the Virgin. Why, then, do you look for nature's order in Christ's body, since the Lord Jesus was Himself brought forth of a Virgin beyond nature? (*Summa Theologica* III, Q. 75, Art. 4).

Put the power of an orator behind a word, and it will thrill and move vast multitudes, like Patrick Henry's "Give me liberty or give me death."

Put the power of a judge behind a word and it will spell the difference between freedom and jail or life and death.

Put the power of God behind a word, and it will pull a universe into being out of a yawning abyss of nothingness.

Take a piece of paper, and put on it the signatures of honorable men, and it will spell the difference between war and peace.

Take simple water and put the power and skill of an engineer behind it, and it will light an entire city.

Take a piece of bread and put the assimilative powers of the human body behind it, and it will be transformed into human flesh and blood.

Put the power of Christ, or His priests, behind: "This is my Body," and it will instantly change the bread into His Body.

Pope Paul VI wrote:

> . . .the Fathers took special care to warn the faithful that in reflecting on this most august Sacrament, they should not trust to their senses, which reach only to appearances of bread and wine, but rather to the words of Christ which have power to transform, change and transmute the bread and wine into His Body and Blood. For, as those same Fathers often said, the power that accomplishes this is the same power by which God Almighty, at the beginning of time, created the world out of nothing" (Encyclical *Mystery of Faith*, 9/3/65).

The first Eucharistic miracle took place in the town of Lanciano in the eighth century. A priest doubting the true presence of Christ in the Eucharist, raised the host during the consecration. The host suddenly changed from the appearance of bread into that of bleeding flesh; and the wine after the consecration changed into five separate globules of blood.

The host-Flesh and wine-Blood are preserved in a beautiful reliquary that can still be seen in the church of St. Longinus in Lanciano, Italy.

In 1970 an investigation of the Miracle of Lanciano, authorized by the local archbishop, revealed that the flesh and blood have remained incorrupt since the eighth century, and that the flesh of the host is heart tissue.

In the year 1263 in the small town of Bolsena, a Bohemian priest who doubted the dogma of transubstantiation celebrated Mass in the church of St. Christine. When he consecrated the host, drops of living blood fell from the host onto the corporal, and each drop had imprinted on it the face of a man. Alarmed, the priest put the blood-soaked corporal in a ciborium and went straight to Pope Urban IV who happened to be nearby at the time in the town of Orvieto. Kneeling before the Pope, the priest confessed his lack of faith and then showed the Holy Father the corporal.

After an investigation, the Pope officially recognized the miracle and in 1264 instituted the feast of Corpus Christi.

The corporal, red with blood, is now kept in a beautiful silver reliquary at Orvieto. Raphael immortalized this miracle in his fresco *The Mass of Bolsena*, covering an entire wall of one of the papal rooms in the Vatican.

A final point: it is well to remember that Christ in the Eucharist is present in the manner of a substance; that is, He is present in the whole host and in each particle. For instance, with ordinary bread, the substance bread is present in the whole loaf, in the slice, and in the crumbs. That is why we must be most careful in receiving Holy Communion to see that no crumbs are lost—Christ is in the whole host and in every particle.

Bishop Samonas of Gaza had come to Jerusalem. A Mohammedan publicly requested him to answer some questions regarding the Blessed Sacrament.

The Mohammedan asked, "How is it possible for bread and wine to become the Body and Blood of Christ?"

The bishop replied, "Your body changes the food you eat into your flesh and blood. Can not God also do what you can do?"

"But, how can Christ be present in His entirety in a small host?"

"The landscape with the blue sky above it," responded the bishop, "is something immense, while your eye is very small. Yet your tiny eye can contain in itself the whole gigantic picture. Is it impossible, then, for Christ to be present in a small piece of bread?"

"How is it possible for the same Christ to be simultaneously present in all your churches?"

"To God nothing is impossible," answered the bishop. "When I speak to a single individual, he hears me. Should I address the same words to 1,000 people, they too would hear the same thing. If I broke a large mirror into a 100 pieces, the image reflected in the large mirror would not be broken; rather there would be the same image in each of the 100 fragments of glass. Why cannot Christ be present in many places at the same time?"

Why is He present?

We have already answered this question in part in the chapter on "Why the Mass?" Christ is present in the Blessed Sacrament to be our companion in the journey of life: to comfort, heal, refresh, strengthen and guide us. He said, *"Come to me all you who labor and are burdened and I will refresh you."* (*Matthew* 11:28). He is there in the Blessed Sacrament so that we might be able to come to Him really and truly for refreshment.

I like this poem *Just for a Minute:*

I remember when I was only four,
Mother would bring me 'round to the store.
And just outside of the Church she'd stand,

And "Come in," she'd say, reaching down
    for my hand,
            "Just for a minute."

And then when I started going to school,
She'd bring me down every day as a rule,
But first the steps to the Church we'd
    climb,
And she'd say: "We'll go in, you've always
    got time,"
            "Just for a minute."

Then I got real big, I mean seven years old,
And I went by myself, but was always
    told:
"When you're passing the Church, don't
    forget to call,
And tell Our Lord about lessons and all,"
            "Just for a minute."

Sometimes I run most of the way,
Or meet some guys and we stop to play,
But I manage to squeeze out time
    enough,
To make the Church where I pant and
    puff,
            "Just for a minute."

And now it's sort of a habit I've got,
In the evening, coming from Casey's lot,
Though it takes me out of my way a bit,
To slip into Church with my hat and mitt.
            "Just for a minute."

But sometimes I see the other fellow
Standing around and I just go yellow,
I pass by the door, but a Voice from
  within,
Seems to say, real sad: "So you wouldn't
  come in,"
       "Just for a minute."

There are things inside of me, bad and
  good,
That nobody knows and nobody could,
Excepting Our Lord, and I like Him to
  know,
And He helps, when in for a visit I go,
       "Just for a minute."

He finds it lonesome when nobody
  comes,
(There are hours upon hours when
  nobody comes)
And He's pleased when anyone passing
  by
Stops in (though it's only a little guy),
       "Just for a minute."

I know what happens when people die,
But I won't be scared, and I'll tell you
  why:
When Our Lord is judging my soul, I feel
He'll remember the times I went to
  kneel,
       "Just for a minute."

A priest saw a certain workingman in the habit of making a pop-in visit to the Blessed Sacrament at noon hour. He literally ran in daily, genuflected, and ran out. When questioned, he explained that he barely had time to do more in his meal hour, but he was sure the Lord would understand.

The priest asked him what prayers he could say in such a swift visit. He answered, "I speak to the Master as to a friend, and for want of time to do more, I just say, 'Jesus, this is Jimmy!'"

Some time afterwards, the priest was summoned on a sick call. The patient was Jimmy. The priest heard his confession and, as he placed the Blessed Sacrament on the tongue of the dying man, the priest distinctly heard the words: "Jimmy, this is Jesus!"

If we go to Jesus in life, He will come to us in death.

Chapter 4

THE SACRIFICE OF THE MASS

The two most important phrases in the Mass are "This is My Body" and "This is the cup of My Blood."

When these words are pronounced by a priest, they make Christ present on our altars by the miracle of transubstantiation.

Now the next two most important words in the Mass are "We offer."

We say the Mass is a sacrifice. What do we mean by sacrifice? Where in the Mass is the sacrifice?

What is a sacrifice?

A sacrifice is giving up something you love for a greater love. For instance, a soldier will give up his life for love of his country. Nathan Hale said, "I regret I have but one life to give for my country."

Therefore a sacrifice has two parts: (1) the giving up part; and (2) the love behind the giving up.

What one gives up can usually be seen; we call this the **exterior sacrifice.**

The love behind the giving up, the *why* one gives up, generally cannot be seen, for you cannot see the heart. This is called the **interior sacrifice.**

Of the two elements in sacrifice, the more important is the second element: the interior sacrifice. The body without the soul is dead; prayers without attention are lip-service; a cathedral without the Blessed Sacrament is a hall. So giving up something without the proper motive renders the gift useless. James Russell Lowell in his *Vision of Sir Launfal* wrote: "The gift without the giver is bare." The heart of sacrifice is the heart. All God asks of us is our hearts: "My child, give me your heart." *"It is love that I desire, not sacrifice. . ."* (*Hosea* 6:6; cp. *Amos* 5:21-24; *Psalm* 51:19).

When Cain and Abel offered their sacrifices, God considered not so much the gifts as the spirit of the giver. God was pleased with Abel's sacrifice, because he was pleased with his spirit. He rejected Cain's sacrifice, because his heart was not good. Later, Jesus rejected the sacrifices of the Scribes and Pharisees, because they were whited sepulchres, offering only lip service to God. When God said, *"Obedience is better than sacrifice,"* (*1 Samuel* 15:22), He meant that the interior sacrifice alone is far better than the exterior sacrifice. An exterior sacrifice without the redeeming interior sacrifice is like counterfeit coin, metal without gold behind it; or it is like a lie, words without truth behind them.

On the contrary, when God asked Abraham to sacrifice his son Isaac, He did not demand Isaac's death once He saw that Abraham's heart was ready to do God's will in all things. As you can have prayers without words, the Blessed Sacrament without cathedral walls, so one can offer sacrifice without destruction.

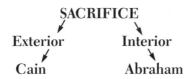

SACRIFICE
Exterior   Interior
Cain   Abraham

The ideal, however is to combine both the exterior and interior sacrifice. Jesus did this on Calvary. He suffered and died—His **Passion;** this constituted the exterior sacrifice or **immolation.** Then He offered up His suffering and death—His **Action;** for He did not die unaware like the unconscious animals sacrificed of old. *"I lay down my life of myself and no man takes it from me"* (*John* 10:18). This offering constituted His interior sacrifice or **oblation**—doing the will of His Father.

As the more important element in all sacrifices is the interior sacrifice, so in the Calvary-sacrifice the more important element was not so much the Passion of Jesus, the laying down of His life, as the Action of Jesus: His laying down His life in obedience to His Father's will. *"He became obedient to death, even to death on a cross. Because of this, God greatly exalted him"* (*Philippians* 2:8-9).

Now the Passion, the immolation of Jesus, ended at 3:00 P.M. on Good Friday. But the Action, the oblation or offering of Jesus, did not end on Good Friday. It preceded it at the Last Supper; it accompanied it on Calvary; and it follows it in Heaven and on earth. Thus the author of *The Letter to the Hebrews* said of the risen Jesus: *"He is a priest forever. . .for he lives forever to make intercession for us"* (*Hebrews* 7:21, 25). In other words, what happened on Calvary is still going on in Heaven. Christ's Action never ceases; nor will it be finished until the Church ceases to be on earth. Always, He is offering for us the death He died on Calvary. *"He continues a priest forever."* His Action is like an unfinished symphony: the Great Composer continues to add offering after offering to the original symphony that was played on Calvary.

Jesus made it possible to bring to earth what is going on in Heaven, when He ordered His apostles and their successors to do what He had done at the Last Supper in remembrance of Himself. Thus at every Mass, priests bring Christ to the altar where He continues what

He is doing at the right hand of the Father.
The Mass is a little bit of Heaven breaking
through on earth; the Mass perpetuates the
sacrificial offering of Calvary.

At Mass the Passion of Jesus is only
represented. How? By the separated pro-
nouncement of the words of consecration.
The priest says, "This is My Body"; then there
is a pause and he says, "This is the cup of My
Blood." If Christ could die, those words would
kill Him. For a sacrament produces what it
signifies: "This is My Body" would bring only
Christ's Body to the altar; and "This is My
Blood" would bring only His Blood. But to
separate body and blood would inflict death.

However, this does not happen, because
Christ can die no more. His Body and Blood,
Soul and Divinity are so united that they can
never be separated. If I have a chain with four
links that cannot be broken, wherever the first
link is the other three will also be. So where
the Body is, there also is the Blood, Soul and
Divinity; and where the Blood is, there also
is the Body, Soul and Divinity.

The Passion of Jesus, therefore, is only represented at the Mass.

The Action of Jesus, however, the heart of the Calvary sacrifice, is **RE-presented** at the Mass. How? By the miracle of transubstantiation. His obedient descent to the altar at the words of consecration prove that the same obedience to the Father's will lasts forever.

There are just three differences between the sacrifice on Calvary and the sacrifice of the Mass. First, on Calvary, the Action of Jesus took place in a bloody and painful manner. For on Calvary reparation for sin was being made, and reparations are always costly and bitter. Secondly, on Calvary graces were being won for all mankind, and to earn requires at least the sweat of one's brow. Thirdly, on Calvary, Jesus trod the winepress alone.

In the Mass, however, the graces already earned on Calvary are being dispensed to sinful man; the Mass applies the fruits of Calvary; thus, as it is a joy to spend what has been earned, the Mass is an unbloody and joyful celebration.

But most importantly, the Mass is not a sacrifice that Christ offers to the Father alone. The Mass is not just His sacrifice, but the Church's. That is why the two most important words after the consecration are "We offer," because they designate our sacrifice. Our sac-

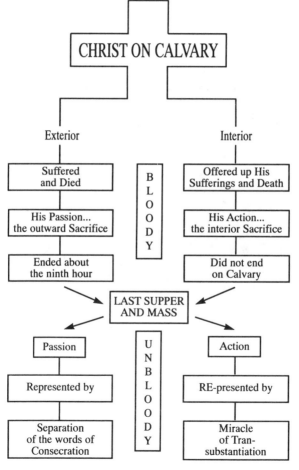

CHRIST ON CALVARY

Exterior

Suffered and Died

His Passion... the outward Sacrifice

Ended about the ninth hour

B L O O D Y

Interior

Offered up His Sufferings and Death

His Action... the interior Sacrifice

Did not end on Calvary

LAST SUPPER AND MASS

Passion

Represented by

Separation of the words of Consecration

U N B L O O D Y

Action

RE-presented by

Miracle of Tran- substantiation

49

rifice is not just Christ, but all the heartaches, the thousand natural shocks that flesh is heir to, the problems, hurts, misunderstandings of the week, which we accept as Jesus accepted His cross, and bring to the altar to offer to the Father with Jesus. Thus the Church prays: "Father look with favor on your Church's offering..." (Eucharistic Prayer III). Here in the "We offer" is our sacrifice in the Mass.

Now Action ought to be linked in some way to life. In philosophy we say, *"Actio sequitur esse";* that is "Action follows existence." One must first *be*, before one can *do*. The thinker must pre-exist his thought; the poet, his poem; the artist, his painting. So life must precede action. Thus with consummate realism, the Church unites the Action of Jesus to His life. Thus the Mass is built upon two pillars: the Liturgy of the Word and the Liturgy of the Eucharist.

The Liturgy of the Word unfolds the life of Christ for us throughout the year. The Liturgy of the Eucharist brings His Action to us at every Mass. Christ's life, which changes from day to day in the liturgy, is happily wedded to the Action of Jesus which is the same yesterday, today and forever.

Every Mass, therefore, challenges us to do two things: (1) to imitate the life of Christ; and (2) to emulate His Action.

We imitate His life by striving to be meek and humble of heart: *"Learn from me, for I am meek and humble of heart" (Matthew* 11:29).

And we emulate His Action whenever we accept our daily crosses, as He did His. His acceptance of suffering made it redemptive; our acceptance of our own sufferings can do the same—fill up what is wanting in His sufferings. Actions speak louder than words. Too often we are full of words, but empty of action. Jesus cursed the fig tree when He found it had no fruit, but only leaves.

Holy Communion with Him, however, enables us to abide in the vine and thus bring forth much fruit. *"Whoever remains in me and I in him will bear much fruit" (John* 15:5).

Chapter 5

THE SACRAMENTAL GRACE OF THE MASS: UNITY

The first most important words in the Mass are the words of consecration, "This is My Body" and "This is My Blood," spoken by a priest, because they effect the great miracle of transubstantiation.

The second most important words are those which follow the Eucharist Acclamation, the words, "We offer." For these words constitute our sacrifice, the sacrifice of the Church.

The third most important element in the Liturgy of the Eucharist is a prayer: "May all of us who share in the Body and Blood of Christ be brought together in unity by the Holy Spirit." This is a prayer to obtain the sacramental grace of the Holy Eucharist, namely, unity. "The Most Holy Eucharist . . . **signifies and effects the unity** of the people of God and achieves the building up of the Body of Christ" (Canon 897).

Twice in the Liturgy of the Eucharist, the priest invokes the Holy Spirit. The first time is just before the consecration. The second is just after the consecration.

The first time the priest invokes the Holy Spirit, he holds his hands over the bread and the wine and asks God the Father to change these into the physical Body and Blood of Christ by sending down the Holy Spirit upon the bread and the wine.

Remember, Mary conceived by the Holy Spirit. At every Mass the Church asks that, just as the Holy Spirit made the Word flesh in the womb of Mary, that He repeat the same miracle and make the risen Christ present in the "womb" of bread and wine. Since God always hears the prayers of His Spouse, the Church, this miracle infallibly follows the words of consecration.

Immediately after these words, the priest holds up the bread for adoration and he himself genuflects; he does the same with the consecrated wine. Then we acclaim Jesus now present on the altar by the Eucharistic Acclamation.

Right after the Acclamation, we offer our sacrifices to the Father together with Jesus'.

Then comes the second invocation of the Holy Spirit. As at the first invocation, when the priest held his hands over the bread and wine and asked the Holy Spirit to turn them into the physical Body and Blood of Christ, so here, when I am the celebrant, I hold my hands over the congregation and pray that it become the mystical body of Christ, the Church.

The prayer that the priest prays here is, "May all of us who share in the Body and Blood of Christ be brought together in unity by the Holy Spirit."

Notice that the priest prays for unity. **Unity is the sacramental grace of the Holy Eucharist.**

At baptism we say we renounce the devil and all his works and pomps. What are the works and pomps of the devil? They are everything that leads to discord, dissension, disunity. The devil is hate and hate is divisive. And how does the devil divide? By lies. Every temptation is a lie. By a lie he robbed our first parents and ourselves of divine life and of paradise. Thus Jesus called him a murderer and a liar.

The Mass counters his lies by the proclamation of the truth in the Liturgy of the Word. Thus Jesus' last prayer for His apostles was: *"Consecrate them in the truth"* (*John* 17:7).

If hatred is divisive, love is unitive. Love makes many one. Thus married love makes two one body. Hence the bond of unity is love.

But what is the source of love?

Love doesn't spring up from inside us, as we already said. We cannot drill deep down into our hearts and expect love to gush forth from us like a geyser. No! Love comes from outside us—we fall in love. Love has to be put into us as gasoline into a car. Whence then comes love? God is love. All love comes from God. Where does God bring love to us? Where is the service station? It is the Mass—the Liturgy of the Eucharist.

God gives us love in the Liturgy of the Eucharist first through the sacrament of love, Holy Communion ("May all of us who receive the Body and Blood of Christ"), then through the God of Love, the Holy Spirit ("be brought together in unity by the Holy Spirit"). *The love of God has been poured out into our hearts through the Holy Spirit that has been given to us" (Romans* 5:5).

Thus St. Augustine said, "The Church makes the Eucharist, by the words of consecration; and the Eucharist makes the Church by making the community one through love given us by Holy Communion and the Holy Spirit."

As the many grains of wheat make the one bread, so we being many become one by the bread of life; and as many grapes make the one wine, so we being many become one by the cup of life. Thus the Holy Eucharist is both the sign and cause of unity; or, as Canon Law

(897) says, "signifies and effects the unity of the people of God."

In the hymn *Lord, Who at Thy First Eucharist* we sing:

O may we all **one** bread, **one** body be,
Through this blest Sacrament of **Unity**.

Every Mass should make each of us a bit more loving, until we all become so filled with love for one another that pagans will see and say, "Look at those Catholics, how they love one another!" In this way the Church becomes visible.

Clement of Alexandria, an early Church Father, stated confidently, "You can always know a pagan by the ugly pleasures in which he indulges, and a heretic by his bickering and quarrelsomeness, and a Christian by his love and happiness."

Because every Mass proclaims the truth and makes us more and more loving persons, transforms us into loving persons, it is the Mass alone that matters. For truth unites people as it did on the first Pentecost with the gift of tongues; and love is the bond of unity, of communion with God and with each other.

Love is the bedrock of marriages, and love comes from the Mass. That is why the Mass is so important for married couples. *"Unless the Lord build the house, they labor in vain who build it" (Psalm 127:1).*

The mission of the Church is to create a "civilization of love" and this can and will be done only through the word of truth proclaimed in the Liturgy of the Word, and through the sacrament of love and the Holy Spirit given in the Liturgy of the Eucharist. *"This is how all will know that you are My disciples, if you have love for one another"* (*John* 13:35). Unity is the mark of the Church and it is also the unmistakable mark of every true follower of Christ, and it can be achieved by frequent and devout participation in the Mass.

*   *   *

Besides being the bond of unity in the Church, the Most Holy Eucharist produces many, many other effects in the soul.

Now a sacrament is a sign which produces what it signifies. Water, for instance, is a sign of cleansing. At Baptism water cleanses the soul of original sin. The sign of Holy Communion is bread and wine. What bread and wine do for the body symbolizes what Holy Communion does for the soul.

1. One of the principal effects of Holy Communion is to augment our union with Christ (*Catholic Catechism* #1391).

Bread unites itself to the one who eats it; so Christ becomes one with him who eats His Flesh and drinks His Blood. St. Cyril of Alexandria wrote, "As two pieces of wax fused together make one, so he who receives Holy Communion is so united with Christ that Christ is in him and he is in Christ." Or as the water mixed with wine at Mass becomes wine, so Holy Communion makes us one with Christ.

Jesus Himself said, *"He who eats my flesh and drinks my blood abides in me, and I in him"* (*John* 6:56).

2. This union with Christ preserves, increases and renews the divine life of grace given us at Baptism (*Catholic Catechism* #1392).

It **preserves** the divine life given us at Baptism, for as St. Thomas commented, "The Eucharist causes a gradual transformation into Christ." And St. Augustine said, "We do not change this food into ourselves as we do with our bodily food; but Jesus Christ changes us into Himself."

It is the bread that makes men strong; the wine that germinates virgins. St. John Chrysostom said that when we return from Holy Communion we are like dragons breathing out fire, so terrible and frightful do we become to the demons of Hell.

It **increases** and **renews** the divine life of grace given us at Baptism. Life given us at Baptism is only a beginning; it is meant to grow just as the human life given at birth is meant to develop. As food nourishes growth, so the Bread of Life nourishes the growth of grace. Just as the mind given us at birth is meant to be developed by education, so the divine life given at Baptism is meant to be developed by Holy Communion.

This growth, or development, consists in two things: first, in a better grasp of the mysteries of our faith, just as education gives one a better grasp of knowledge; and secondly, a deeper implanting of the divine life in the soul so that it becomes almost impossible to lose it. A sapling can easily be uprooted, but when it develops into an oak, then it is difficult to uproot it.

3. St. Pius X declared that the very substance chosen for the Eucharist—bread—indicates that Jesus wished the Eucharist to be a necessary, universal, common and daily food.

Necessary, that is, irreplaceable. Jesus said, *"Take and eat". . ."Take and drink."* Without food one dies; without the Eucharist one will lose the life of grace and die spiritually. For Jesus said, *"This is the bread that comes down from heaven so that one may eat of it and not die"* (*John* 6:50).

Universal, that is, known by everyone and eaten everywhere by everyone.

Common, that is, within the reach of everybody, rich and poor, the great and the little ones.

Daily, that is, a food that should be received every day. The Church commands that we go to Holy Communion at least once a year under pain of mortal sin. Jesus and the Holy Father, St. Pius X, spoke of *"daily bread."* This, however, is not a command but a piece of excellent advice.

After the Protestant Reformation, there followed a terrible heresy called Jansenism. The heresy maintained that only the good could go to Holy Communion. *Sancta sanctis—* "holy things to the holy." As a result frequent Holy Communion fell off.

It was the great St. Pius X who reminded the faithful of the true teaching of the Church; namely, that the Eucharist is not a reward, but a food; a remedy. Jesus did not come to call the just but sinners: *"Those who are well do not need a physician, but the sick do"* (*Mark* 2:17). The pope opened up this sacrament to children. He said, "Let them go to Communion before they know sin; and to confession before they know fear."

4. St. Pius X insisted on frequent communion from the earliest age, because, just as a well-fed body can ward off diseases, so frequent Holy Communion wipes away venial

sins. Christ in us revives love in us and enables us to break away from our disordered
passions. In fact if we receive Holy Communion frequently, the habit of venial sins and our
affection for them will be eradicated,
uprooted.

5. Then, too, frequent Holy Communion
worthily received preserves us from future
mortal sins. Jesus Himself said, *"Whoever eats
this bread shall not die"* (*John* 6:50). For the
closer we come to Christ the harder it is to
turn our backs on Him (Cf. *Catholic Catechism* #1394-5).

Two classes of people ought to avail themselves of Holy Communion: the bad that they
might become good; and the good that they
might become better.

6. Holy Communion, as we have already
explained, builds up the unity of the Church,
just as eating together builds up friendship.
Aristotle said that to become friends two persons must eat a bushel of salt together. At a
meal we eat only a pinch of salt. To eat a
bushel would require thousands of meals
together. So frequent Holy Communions, by
the thousands, are needed to build up friend-
ships, unity in the Church. As St. Paul said,
*"Because there is one bread, we who are many
are one body, for we all partake of the one
bread"* (*1 Corinthians* 10:17).

7. Holy Communion is a pledge of the life to come.

"Whoever eats my flesh and drinks my blood has eternal life and I will raise him on the last day" (*John* 6:54).

O sacred banquet in which Christ is
   received as food,
the memory of His Passion is renewed,
the soul is filled with grace
and a pledge of the life to come is given.

8. God gave man *"wine to gladden his heart"* (*Psalm* 104:15). The final effect of Holy Communion is **joy.** *"Come to Me all you who labor and are burdened and I will refresh you."*

During the terrible persecution of Christians in Vietnam under the Emperor Tu-Doc, he realized the power of Holy Communion and gave the orders, "Let a guard be put at the door of the Christians' prison, to prevent their obtaining a certain enchanted bread which renders them insensible to pain and makes them die with joy."

*   *   *

We don't have to be saints to receive Holy Communion. The Church lays down only two conditions: to be in **the state of grace** and **to fast at least one hour before Holy Communion.**

We have to be in the state of grace; that is, spiritually alive, for you don't feed a corpse. A corpse cannot eat or drink. To receive Holy Communion in mortal sin would constitute another mortal sin—would be a sacrilege, that is, the abuse of a sacred thing, and nothing is so sacred as the Holy Eucharist. St. Paul wrote, "*A person should examine himself, and so eat the bread and drink the cup. For anyone who eats and drinks without discerning the body, eats and drinks judgment on himself*" (1 Corinthians 11:28-29). The *Catechism of the Catholic Church* says, "Sacrilege is a grave sin especially when committed against the Eucharist, for Christ is present here for us" (#2120). To St. Bridget Jesus said, "There does not exist on earth a punishment which is great enough to punish it [a sacrilege] sufficiently!"

To remove deadly sin, Jesus gave us the sacrament of Reconciliation. However, even when there is not serious sin, confession is good to render a soul more pure and to adorn it with a more beautiful wedding garment to take its place at the table of the angels. We wash our hands before meals; we don't wait until they are blackened and dirtied beyond recognition. So confession, even when we are not conscious of mortal sin, is always a good preparation for Holy Communion.

St. Camillus de Lellis never celebrated Mass without first going to confession, because he wanted at least to "dust off" his soul.

After receiving Holy Communion, do three things: **T W A.**

T—thank God the Father for sending us His Son.

W—welcome God the Son. Take time; if a guest comes to your house, courtesy and good manners demand that you welcome him.

A—ask God the Holy Spirit for the needs of your body and soul and the needs of those near and dear to you.

One Holy Communion is of greater value than an ecstasy, rapture or vision.

"If angels could envy, they would envy us for Holy Communion"—St. Pius X.

Chapter 6

WHAT IS THE SUNDAY OBLIGATION?

Regarding the Sunday obligation, the law of the Church says:

> On Sundays and other holy days of obligation the faithful are bound to participate in the Mass; they are also to abstain from those labors and business concerns which impede the worship to be rendered to God, the joy which is proper to the Lord's Day, or the proper relaxation of mind and body (Canon 1247).

The law of the Church imposes two obligations concerning Sundays. The first regards Sunday Mass. In the 1917 Code of Canon Law the phrase for Sunday Mass was "obligation to hear holy Mass." In the Revised Code (1983) the phrase was made much stronger: "the faithful are **bound** to participate in the Mass." The faithful are bound! Sunday Mass is not just an obligation; it is a serious obligation—one that binds!

The second command regards the Sunday rest: the faithful are to abstain from labors and business concerns that might impede worship, joy and relaxation of mind and body. In the old Code the focus was on the kinds of **work** forbidden. In the new Code the attention is directed to the **purpose** of the celebration of the Lord's Day and the joy and the leisure necessary for that celebration.

✳   ✳   ✳

Regarding Sunday Mass. The obligation of participating in Mass on Sunday goes back to the Lord Himself. On the first Easter Jesus celebrated Mass while He was at table with the disciples at Emmaus (*Luke* 24:30). When St. Paul was at Troas, St. Luke writes, "*On the first day of the week when we gathered to break bread, Paul spoke. . .*" (*Acts* 20:7). Apparently at this early date it was the custom to gather together on the first day of the week, Sunday, to break bread, that is, to celebrate Mass. St. John tells us that his vision regarding the letters to the churches of Asia Minor took place on the Lord's day, Sunday. "*I was caught up in spirit on the Lord's day. . . .*" (*Revelation* 1:10).

Thus Vatican II said in its *Constitution on the Sacred Liturgy:*

> By an apostolic tradition which took its origin from the very day of Christ's

resurrection, the Church celebrates the paschal mystery every eighth day; with good reason this, then bears the name of the Lord's day. . . . For on this day Christ's faithful should come together into one place so that, by hearing the word of God and taking part in the Eucharist, they may call to mind the passion, the resurrection, and the glorification of the Lord Jesus, and may thank God who "has begotten us again, through the resurrection of Jesus Christ". . . .

Hence the Lord's day is the original feast day, and it should be proposed to the piety of the faithful and taught to them in such a way that it may become in fact a day of joy and of freedom from work (#106).

Why does the Church wish us to celebrate the Lord's day by participating in the Mass?

One reason is that we need power from Jesus to keep our faith. Deliberately missing Sunday Mass without a reason week in and week out leads to a loss of faith.

It is significant that the *Catechism of the Catholic Church* has four illustrations in it, at the beginning of each of the four Parts into which it is divided. The illustration introducing the Part on the sacraments is a fresco from the catacomb of Saints Marcellinus and Peter in Rome, dating from the beginning of the fourth century A.D.

The scene depicts the encounter of Jesus with the woman with the hemorrhage. This woman, who had suffered for many years, was healed by touching the cloak of Jesus through the power that *"had gone forth from Him"* (Cf. *Mark* 5:25-34).

The sacraments are as it were **"powers that go forth" from the Body of Christ** to heal the wounds of sin and to give us the new life of Christ (Cf. *Catholic Catechism* #1116). Of no sacrament is this more true than of the Most Holy Eucharist. To neglect it is to cut oneself off from the power of Christ, needed to live the Christian life. Lest we forget, the Church binds us to participate in the Eucharist at least once a week.

Secondly, we, as individuals, need a support community. The plant needs the soil; the child needs the family; the Christian needs the Christian family. Thus the author of *The Letter to the Hebrews* told the early Christians, *"We should not stay away from our assembly, as is the custom of some, but encourage one another. . ."* (*Hebrews* 10:25).

The Mass is not like going to a movie, where people can enjoy themselves and never look at anybody else. Nor is it like a cafeteria, where everyone can pick and choose what he or she likes, regardless of everyone else. No, the Mass is what the Last Supper was—a gathering of friends, of people who care for each other. At this table Christ gives us courage, strength and love; and this, plus the example of all the others present, empowers us to go out into the world and be what we are supposed to be. In Alcoholics Anonymous, people humbly admit their weakness; and each one accepts and supports the other; and thus all are strengthened by the community.

Thirdly, we ought to go to Sunday Mass to pay our bills. We "owe" God. Not a very appealing reason, it's true, but it's rock bottom. We owe God for our life. We depend on Him for life, more than the electric light depends on the current of electricity, more than the sunbeam depends on the sun, more than the baby in its mother's womb depends on its mother. If it is wrong to refuse to pay what you owe the baker for the bread with which you nourish your life, it is a greater wrong to refuse to pay what you owe God for the life that the bread nourishes.

Therefore, it is right and just always and everywhere to praise and to thank God. To **praise** God, for He is so good in Himself. Freely, out of pure love, He created us to be the beneficiaries of His blessings. To **thank** God, for He is so good to us. He sent His Son to die for us to save us.

There is deep pathos in Jesus' words, *"Ten were cleansed, were they not? Where are the other nine?"* (*Luke* 17:17). Someone said, there are not seven capital sins; there are eight, and the first is ingratitude. And the terrible tragedy, as Shakespeare said, "One good deed lying thankless slaughters a thousand others waiting upon it."

We have all heard the time-worn excuses some people give for not going to church on Sunday: "They made me go as a child"; "Those who go to church on Sunday are hypocrites—they think they are better than everybody else"; "None of my friends go anymore"; "All the Church talks about is money"; "The Mass is boring—I get nothing out of it"; and so on and on.

Well, a pastor, parodying these excuses, wrote a satirical piece in his parish bulletin titled *Reasons Why I Never Wash.*

I was made to wash as a child.
People who wash are hypocrites: they think they are cleaner than other people.
I used to wash, but it got so boring so I stopped.
There are so many different kinds of soap, I could never decide which one was right.
I still wash on special occasions, like Christmas and Easter.

None of my friends wash.

I'm still young; when I'm older and have got a bit dirtier, I might start washing.

People who make soap are only after your money.

Regarding the Sunday rest. The whole idea of the Sunday rest originated at first to allow people to worship God. Constantine the Great closed all public buildings at 9:00 A.M. on Sundays so that people could worship God.

Taking time off to celebrate the Eucharist began to give the Sunday an air of joy and relaxation. It reflected the peace, love and joy that flooded the worshipers because of what Jesus had done for them. He died for us; greater love than this no man has. And He comes to us at every Mass to share with us His life and love and peace. So the celebration radiated joy and peace.

We catch this spirit of joy and peace and relaxation at Christmas and on Easter. But that same spirit should pervade every Sunday for every Sunday is "a little Easter" and "a little Christmas."

Later on, the time off for Sunday Mass was extended from an hour to the entire day, for the Lord had said, *"Keep holy the Lord's day"*—not just an hour. And the law of the Church says we can do this if we abstain from those labors and business concerns which impede worship, joy or relaxation.

The focus, as we said, was not on the kinds of works that are prohibited on the Lord's day, but on the purpose. The abstinence from work applies only to those tasks that impede worship, joy or relaxation. One of the greatest attacks on this law is Sunday shopping. I feel this is a great wrong because it forces people to work on Sunday. The exception, of course, is for those services that are necessary, like the fire and police departments, the hospital staff, and so on. As a rule, there is no reason for stores to be open on Sunday—except greed!

Once there was a man who had nothing. God gave him seven apples. Two apples, He gave him for food. The man ate the first two apples. God gave him two apples to trade for clothing. He traded these for clothing to cover his body. God gave him the third pair of apples to trade for shelter from sun and rain. He traded these two for shelter from sun and rain.

God gave him the seventh apple so he would have something to give back to God in gratitude for the other six.

But the man held up the seventh apple and admired it. It seemed larger and juicier than all the others. He knew in his heart that this was the apple God expected him to use as a gift of gratitude for the other six. But the seventh apple seemed better than the others. And, he reasoned, God has all the other apples in the world, so the man ate the seventh apple, and gave God the core.

God gives us seven days. One He expects us to use to thank Him. But so often we Sunday shop, skip Mass, and give Him the core.

Our Bodies Need the Sunday Rest

Suppose there were no days but schooldays. Jack would indeed become a dull boy. Suppose there were no days but workdays. Jack's father and mother would soon become weary and ill. For God *"knows how we are formed"* (*Psalm* 103:14). He knows what is best for the human body; what it can take and give. Long before labor unions agitated for a forty-hour week, God—by His Sabbath rest and His Church by her Sunday rest—had given man the greatest labor law in history.

Man can try to alter this, but inevitably he becomes the loser. During the French Revolution, for instance, when godless men tried to abolish the Sunday and establish a ten-day week, it wasn't long before people began clamoring, "Give us back our Sunday." In World War II, under the stress of total war, our country instituted a seven-day work week.

Before long, modern industry was plagued with the problem of absenteeism.

The most perfect machines will not run without rest; and men are not machines, they are flesh and blood, not iron and coal. The heart attacks, nervous breakdowns, ulcers and sleeplessness so characteristic of our modern society are but the price of high-pressure industry. As the earth needs the sun, man's body needs rest at least on Sundays.

Also, for man to get complete rest and relaxation, the day of rest must be a common one. To give a rest day on a Monday to some, or to some other day of the week when everybody else is at work, does not serve the purpose of rest. The day of rest must be one in common for the entire community. Only on a common day of rest can people get together with other people—the condition necessary for celebration and relaxation.

The Soul Needs the Sunday Rest

Man, of course, is more than a body. He has a soul destined for life beyond this life. Without the Sunday rest, how long would man remember this? Sunday is a reminder, a *memento homo*, that we have not here a lasting city, but look for one that is to come. It tells us that just as a day of rest follows every six days of labor, so, too, when the business of life is done, there will follow a Sunday of eternal rest.

Sunday is an invitation to come apart from the hustle and bustle of life and rest a while with Christ, to leave the things of earth for just a day that we may devote ourselves to the things beyond the earth.

Leo XIII wrote:

> The cessation from work and labor on Sundays...is not to be understood as mere idleness. Much less must it be an occasion for vicious indulgence;... it should be rest from labor, hallowed by religion.

> Rest (combined with religious observance) disposes man to forget for a while the business of his everyday life, to turn his thoughts to things heavenly, and to render the worship he so strictly owes to God. It is this, above all, which is the reason and motive of Sunday rest—a rest sanctioned by God's great law: *"Remember thou keep holy the Sabbath day,"* and taught by His own mysterious "rest" after the creation of man: *"He rested on the seventh day from all He had done"* (*Rerum Novarum,* #58).

If man denies God one day a week, it will not be long before he will deny God. If he refuses to rest from his labors, he will soon refuse to labor for the rest that is eternal. Nations that do not observe Sunday have a citizenry enchained in slavery and misery. On a smaller scale, the individuals who do not observe Sunday have a week of days in which everything seems to go wrong.

A Sunday well spent
    Brings a week of content
And health for the toils of tomorrow.

But a Sunday profaned,
    Whate'er may be gained
Is a certain forerunner of sorrow.

"For this is the day the Lord hath made, let us be glad and rejoice therein" (*Psalm* 118:24).

Appendix I

SCRIPTURES REFERRING TO THE EUCHARIST

During the meal Jesus took bread, blessed it, broke it, and gave it to his disciples. "Take this and eat it," he said, "this is my body." Then he took a cup, gave thanks, and gave it to them. "All of you must drink from it," he said, "for this is my blood, the blood of the covenant, to be poured out in behalf of many for the forgiveness of sins. I tell you, I will not drink this fruit of the vine from now until the day when I drink it new with you in my Father's reign" (Matthew 26:26-30). Also, (Mark 14:22-25) and (Luke 22:14-20).

*   *   *

"I myself am the living bread come down from heaven. If anyone eats this bread he shall live forever; the bread I will give is my flesh, for the life of the world." At this the Jews quarreled among themselves, saying, "How can he give us his flesh to eat?" Thereupon Jesus said to them: "Let me solemnly assure you, if you do not eat the flesh of the Son of Man and drink

his blood, you have no life in you. He who feeds on my flesh and drinks my blood has life eternal, and I will raise him up on the last day. For my flesh is real food and my blood real drink. The man who feeds on my flesh and drinks my blood remains in me, and I in him. Just as the Father who has life sent me and I have life because of the Father, so the man who feeds on me will have life because of me. This is the bread that came down from heaven. Unlike your ancestors who ate and died nonetheless, the man who feeds on this bread shall live forever" (*John* 6:51-58).

*　　　*　　　*

I received from the Lord what I handed on to you, namely, that the Lord Jesus on the night in which he was betrayed took bread, and after he had given thanks, broke it and said, "This is my body, which is for you. Do this in remembrance of me." In the same way, after the supper, he took the cup, saying, "This cup is the new covenant in my blood. Do this, whenever you drink it, in remembrance of me." Every time, then, you eat this bread and drink this cup, you proclaim the death of the Lord until he comes! This means that whoever eats the bread or drinks the cup of the Lord unworthily sins against the body and blood of the Lord. A man should examine himself first; only then should he eat of the bread and drink of the cup. He who eats and drinks without recognizing the *body eats and drinks a judgment on himself. That is why many among you are sick and infirm, and why so many are dying. If we were to examine ourselves, we would not be falling under judgment in this way* (1 Corinthians 11:23-31).

Other Scriptures Referring to the Eucharist

Genesis 14:18; *Psalm* 104:13-15; *Psalm* 116:13, 17; *Malachi* 1:11; *Matthew* 14:13-21; *Mark* 8:14-21; *Luke* 24:13-35; *John* 2:1-11; *John* 13:1-17, 34-35; *Acts* 2:42-47; *Acts* 20:7-11; *1 Corinthians* 10:16-17; *Galatians* 2:20; *Hebrews* 7:25-27; *Hebrews* 9:11-14; *1 Peter* 2:5.

Appendix II

CATECHISM OF THE CATHOLIC CHURCH

In part, the Sacrament of the Eucharist is further defined in the Catechism in the following paragraphs:

1406 Jesus said: "I am the living bread that came down from heaven; if any one eats of this bread, he will live for ever; . . . he who eats my flesh and drinks my blood has eternal life and . . . abides in me, and I in him" (*John* 6:51, 54, 56).

1407 The Eucharist is the heart and the summit of the Church's life, for in it Christ associates his Church and all her members with his sacrifice of praise and thanksgiving offered once for all on the cross to his Father; by this sacrifice he pours out the graces of salvation on his Body which is the Church.

1409 The Eucharist is the memorial of Christ's Passover, that is, of the work of salvation accomplished by the life, death, and resurrection of Christ, a work made present by the liturgical action.

1410 It is Christ himself, the eternal high priest of the New Covenant who, acting through the ministry of the priests, offers the Eucharistic sacrifice. And it is the same Christ, really present under the species of bread and wine, who is the offering of the Eucharistic sacrifice.

1411 Only validly ordained priests can preside at the Eucharist and consecrate the bread and wine so that they become the Body and Blood of the Lord.

1412 The essential signs of the Eucharistic sacrament are wheat bread and grape wine, on which the blessing of the Holy Spirit is invoked and the priest pronounces the words of consecration spoken by Jesus during the Last Supper: "This is my body which will be given up for you....This is the cup of my blood...."

1413 By the consecration the transubstantiation of the bread and wine into the Body and Blood of Christ is brought about. Under the consecrated species of bread and wine Christ himself, living and glorious, is present in a true, real, and substantial manner: his Body and his Blood, with his soul and his divinity (cf. Council of Trent: DS 1640; 1651).

1414 As sacrifice, the Eucharist is also offered in reparation for the sins of the living and the dead and to obtain spiritual or temporal benefits from God.

1415 Anyone who desires to receive Christ in Eucharistic communion must be in the state of grace. Anyone aware of having sinned mortally must not receive communion without having received absolution in the sacrament of penance.

1416 Communion with the Body and Blood of Christ increases the communicant's union with the Lord, forgives his venial sins, and preserves him from grave sins. Since receiving this sacrament strengthens the bonds of charity between the communicant and Christ, it also reinforces the unity of the Church as the Mystical Body of Christ.

1418 Because Christ himself is present in the sacrament of the altar, he is to be honored with the worship of adoration. "To visit the Blessed Sacrament is. . .a proof of gratitude, an expression of love, and a duty of adoration toward Christ our Lord" (Paul VI, *Mysterium Fidei* 66).

Appendix III

VATICAN II DOCUMENTS

The documents of Vatican II provide extensive material relating to the Church's position on the Mass. In the *Constitution On The Sacred Liturgy,* in the introduction, it states:

For the liturgy, "through which the work of our redemption is accomplished," most of all in the divine sacrifice of the eucharist, is the outstanding means whereby the faithful may express in their lives, and manifest to others, the mystery of Christ and the real nature of the true Church. It is of the essence of the Church that she be both human and divine, visible and yet invisibly equipped, eager to act and yet intent on contemplation, present in this world and yet not at home in it; and she is all these things in such wise that in her the human is directed and subordinated to the divine, the visible likewise to the invisible, action to contemplation, and this present world to that city yet to come, which we seek. While the liturgy daily builds up those who are within into a holy temple of the Lord, into a dwelling place for God in the Spirit, to the mature measure of the fullness of Christ, at the same time it marvelously strengthens their power to preach Christ, and thus shows forth the Church to those who are outside as a sign lifted up among the nations, under which the scattered children of God may be gathered together, until there is one sheepfold and one shepherd.

Chapter 1, under the title of, *The Nature of the Sacred Liturgy and Its Importance in the Church's Life,* states:

God who "wills that all men be saved and come to the knowledge of the truth" (*1 Timothy* 2:4), "who in many and various ways spoke in times past to the fathers by the prophets" (*Hebrews* 1:1), when the fullness of time had come sent His Son, the Word made flesh, anointed by the Holy Spirit, to preach the gospel to the poor, to heal the contrite of heart, to be a "bodily and spiritual medicine," the Mediator between God and man. For His humanity, united with the person of the Word, was the instrument of our salvation. Therefore in Christ "the perfect achievement of our reconciliation came forth, and the fullness of divine worship was given to us."

The wonderful works of God among the people of the Old Testament were but a prelude to the work of Christ the Lord in redeeming mankind and giving perfect glory to God. He achieved His task principally by the paschal mystery of His blessed passion, resurrection from the dead, and glorious ascension, whereby "dying, he destroyed our death and, rising, he restored our life." For it was from the side of Christ as He slept the sleep of death upon the cross that there came forth "the wondrous sacrament of the whole Church."

Just as Christ was sent by the Father, so also He sent the apostles, filled with the Holy Spirit. This He did that, by preaching the gospel to every creature, they might proclaim that the Son of God, by His death and resurrection, had freed us from the power of Satan and from death, and brought us into the kingdom of His Father. His purpose also was that they might accomplish the work of salvation which they had proclaimed, by means of sacrifice and sacraments, around which the entire liturgical life revolves. Thus by baptism men are plunged into the paschal mystery of Christ: they die with Him, are buried with Him, and rise with Him; they receive the spirit of adoption as sons "in which we cry: Abba, Father" (*Romans* 8:15), and thus become true adorers whom the Father seeks. In like manner, as often as they eat the supper of the Lord they proclaim the death of the Lord until He comes. For that reason, on the very day of Pentecost, when the Church appeared before the world, "those who received the word" of Peter "were baptized." And "they continued steadfastly in the teaching of the apostles and in the communion of the breaking of bread and in prayers. . . praising

God and being in favor with all the people" (*Acts* 2:41-47). From that time onwards the Church has never failed to come together to celebrate the paschal mystery: reading those things "which were in all the scriptures concerning him" (*Luke* 24:27), celebrating the eucharist in which "the victory and triumph of his death are again made present," and at the same time giving thanks "to God for his unspeakable gift" (*2 Corinthians* 9:15) in Christ Jesus, "in praise of his glory" (*Ephesians* 1:12), through the power of the Holy Spirit.

To accomplish so great a work, Christ is always present in His Church, especially in her liturgical celebrations. He is present in the sacrifice of the Mass, not only in the person of His minister, "the same now offering, through the ministry of priests, who formerly offered himself on the cross," but especially under the eucharistic species. By His power He is present in the sacraments, so that when a man baptizes it is really Christ Himself who baptizes. He is present in His word, since it is He Himself who speaks when the holy scriptures are read in the Church. He is present, lastly, when the Church prays and sings, for He promised: "Where two or three are gathered together in my name, there am I in the midst of them" (*Matthew* 18:20).

Christ indeed always associates the Church with Himself in this great work wherein God is perfectly glorified and men are sanctified. The Church is His beloved Bride who calls to her Lord, and through Him offers worship to the Eternal Father.

Rightly, then, the liturgy is considered as an exercise of the priestly office of Jesus Christ. In the liturgy the sanctification of the man is signified by signs perceptible to the senses, and is effected in a way which corresponds with each of these signs; in the liturgy the whole public worship is performed by the Mystical Body of Jesus Christ, that is, by the Head and His members.

From this it follows that every liturgical celebration, because it is an action of Christ the priest and of His Body which is the Church, is a sacred action surpassing all others; no other action of the Church can equal its efficacy by the same title and to the same degree.

The sacred liturgy does not exhaust the entire activity of the Church. Before men can come to the liturgy they must be called to faith and to conversion: "How then are they to call upon him in whom they have not yet believed? But how are they to believe him whom they have not heard? And how are they to hear if no one preaches? And how are men to preach unless they be sent?" (*Romans* 10:14-15) . . . .

Nevertheless the liturgy is the summit toward which the activity of the Church is directed; at the same time it is the font from which all her power flows. For the aim and object of apostolic works is that all who are made sons of God by faith and baptism should come together to praise God in the midst of His Church, to take part in the sacrifice, and to eat the Lord's supper.

The liturgy in its turn moves the faithful, filled with "the paschal sacraments," to be "one in holiness"; it prays that "they may hold fast in their lives to what they have grasped by their faith"; the renewal in the eucharist of the covenant between the Lord and man draws the faithful into the compelling love of Christ and sets them on fire. From the liturgy, therefore, and especially from the eucharist, as from a font, grace is poured forth upon us; and the sanctification of men in Christ and the glorification of God, to which all other activities of the Church are directed as toward their end, is achieved in the most efficacious possible way.

But in order that the liturgy may be able to produce its full effects, it is necessary that the faithful come to it with proper dispositions, that their minds should be attuned to their voices, and that they should cooperate with divine grace lest they receive it in vain. Pastors of souls must therefore realize that, when the liturgy is celebrated, something more is required than the mere observation of the laws governing valid and licit celebration; it is their duty also to ensure that the faithful take part fully aware of what they are doing, actively engaged in the rite, and enriched by its effects.

The spiritual life, however, is not limited solely to participation in the liturgy. The Christian is indeed called to pray with his brethren, but he must also enter into his chamber to pray to the Father, in secret; yet more, according to the teaching of the Apostle, he should pray without ceasing. We learn from the same Apostle that we must always bear about in our body the dying of Jesus, so that the life also of Jesus may be made manifest in our bodily frame. This is why we ask the Lord in the sacrifice of the Mass that, "receiving the offering of the spiritual victim," he may fashion us for himself "as an eternal gift."

In Chapter 2, *The Most Sacred Mystery of the Eucharist,* we read:

At the Last Supper, on the night when He was betrayed, our Saviour instituted the eucharistic sacrifice of His Body and Blood. He did this in order to perpetuate the sacrifice of the Cross throughout the centuries until He should come again, and so to entrust to His beloved spouse, the Church, a memorial of His death and resurrection: a sacrament of love, a sign of unity, a bond of charity, a paschal banquet in which Christ is eaten, the mind is filled with grace, and a pledge of future glory is given to us.

The Church, therefore, earnestly desires that Christ's faithful, when present at this mystery of faith, should not be there as strangers or silent spectators; on the contrary, through a good understanding of the rites and prayers they should take part in the sacred action conscious of what they are doing, with devotion and full collaboration. They should be instructed by God's word and be nourished at the table of the Lord's body; they should give thanks to God; by offering the Immaculate Victim, not only through the hands of the priest, but also with him, they should learn also to offer themselves; through Christ the Mediator, they should be drawn day by day into ever more perfect union with God and with each other, so that finally God may be all in all.

Books
By Rev. Albert J. M. Shamon

Our Lady Teaches About Prayer at Medjugorje

Our Lady Says: Let Holy Mass Be Your Life

Our Lady Says: Monthly Confession—
Remedy for the West

Our Lady Teaches About Sacramentals
and Blessed Objects

Our Lady Says: Pray the Creed

Three Steps to Sanctity

The Power of the Rosary

Preparing for the Third Millennium

Our Lady Says: Love People

The Ten Commandments of God

Behind the Mass

Apocalypse—The Book For Our Times

Firepower Through Confirmation

Genesis: The Book of Origins

Exodus: Road To Freedom

A Graphic Life of Jesus the Christ

For additional information, contact **THE RIEHLE FOUNDATION,** distributor of Catholic books.

Write: **THE RIEHLE FOUNDATION**
 P.O. Box 7
Milford, OH 45150-0007
513-576-0032

THE RIEHLE FOUNDATION...

The Riehle Foundation is a non-profit, tax-exempt, charitable organization that exists to produce and/or distribute Catholic material to anyone, anywhere.

The Foundation is dedicated to the Mother of God and her role in the salvation of mankind. We believe that this role has not diminished in our time, but, on the contrary has become all the more apparent in this the era of Mary as recognized by Pope John Paul II, whom we strongly support.

During the past five years the foundation has distributed over four million books, films, rosaries, bibles, etc. to individuals, parishes, and organizations all over the world. Additionally, the foundation sends materials to missions and parishes in a dozen foreign countries.

Donations forwarded to The Riehle Foundation for the materials distributed provide our sole support. We appreciate your assistance, and request your prayers.

IN THE SERVICE OF JESUS AND MARY
All for the honor and glory of God!

The Riehle Foundation
P.O. Box 7
Milford, OH 45150

Faith Publishing Company

Faith Publishing Company has been organized as a service for the publishing and distribution of materials that reflect Christian values, and in particular, the teachings of the Catholic Church.

It is dedicated to publication of only those materials that reflect such values.

Faith Publishing Company also publishes books for The Riehle Foundation. The Foundation is a non-profit, tax-exempt producer and distributor of Catholic books and materials worldwide and also supplies hospital and prison ministries, churches, and mission organizations.

For more information on the publications of Faith Publishing Company, contact:

Faith Publishing Company
P.O. BOX 237
MILFORD, OHIO 45150